DIVINE ECHOES

RECONCILING PRAYER WITH THE UNCONTROLLING LOVE OF GOD

INDIVIDUAL OR SMALL GROUP STUDY GUIDE

MARK GREGORY KARRIS

All rights reserved. No part of this book may be used or reproduced, stored in a retrieval system, or transmitted in any form or by any means, electronic, mechanical, photocopying, recording, scanning, or otherwise, without written permission from the publisher except in the case of brief quotations embodied in critical articles and reviews. Permission for wider usage of this material can be obtained through Quoir by emailing permission@quoir.com.

Copyright © 2018 by Mark Gregory Karris.

First Edition

Cover design and layout by Rafael Polendo (polendo.net)

All Scripture quotations, unless otherwise indicated, are from the Holy Bible, New International Version®, NIV®. Copyright © 1973, 1978, 1984, 2011 by Biblica, Inc.™ Used by permission of Zondervan. All rights reserved worldwide. www.zondervan.com.

Scripture quotations marked KJV are from the King James Version of the Bible. Scripture quotations marked NLT are from the New Living Translation Version of the Bible, *Holy Bible: New Living Translation*. Wheaton, IL: Tyndale House Publishers, 2004. Print. Scripture quotations marked NRSV are from the New Revised Standard Version of the Bible, copyright © 1989 by the National Council of the Churches of Christ in the U.S.A. Used by permission. All rights reserved.

ISBN 978-1-938480-27-0

This volume is printed on acid free paper and meets ANSI Z39.48 standards.

Printed in the United States of America

Published by Quoir
Orange, California

www.quoir.com

TABLE OF CONTENTS

A Note from Mark 5

Introduction 7

Chapter 1 9
My Journey Into Petitionary Prayer

Chapter 2 13
What Are the Mechanics of Prayer?

Chapter 3 17
Unforeseen Theological and Philosophical Pitfalls of Petitionary Prayer

Chapter 4 21
Critical Empirical and Experiential Concerns About Petitionary Prayer

Chapter 5 25
Petitionary Prayer and the Bible

Chapter 6 29
God's Perfect, Uncontrolling Love

Chapter 7 33
God's Open-Door Policy

Chapter 8 37
Principles of Conspiring Prayer

Chapter 9 41
Conspiring Prayer in Action

Appendix 1 45
Write Your Own Conspiring Prayer

A NOTE FROM MARK

Welcome to this study guide for *Divine Echoes*! I am very excited that you get to journey through these thought-provoking questions. It is not too often that we take the time to contemplate a sacred practice that has been around for millennia—a practice that many of us frequently engage in but seldom question. As I share in my book, although I am biased in my own commitment to *conspiring prayer* and the foundational theodicy it is built upon, my desire is for you to work through your own theology of prayer. May these questions and the conversations that come from them take you to rewarding spiritual and theological destinations you could not have imagined.

HOW TO USE THIS STUDY GUIDE

While individuals may find this study guide enormously helpful, I encourage readers to use it in small groups. Wrestling through difficult questions as a community brings about new adventures of thought and reflection that working through this guide alone may not. To get the most from this experience, find one, two, or more people to engage the book and study guide with.

This study guide, following the book, has nine chapters. Each set of questions comes from the respective chapter in the book. Although it is helpful for each group member to have read the relevant chapter of *Divine Echoes* prior to the study, it is possible to engage with the material regardless. While each chapter builds on the next, feel free to skip around to topics that may interest you.

Be prayerful. Take risks. Share openly and honestly. Avoid judging or criticizing one another. And enjoy the adventure!

Finally, I'd love to hear from you if you are using this resource; and do drop me a line to let me know how the material might be improved for the future.

—**Mark Gregory Karris**
mark@conspiringprayer.com
January 2018

INTRODUCTION

1. Can you describe a time when you know, without a shadow of a doubt, that God answered your prayers?

2. Dallas Willard writes, "The idea that everything would happen exactly as it does regardless of whether we pray or not is a specter that haunts the minds of many who sincerely profess belief in God." Have you ever been haunted by the question of whether or not prayer works?

3. Have you ever been disappointed by unanswered prayer? Have you shared your disappointment with someone you trust? If not, what has prevented you from sharing?

4. Read the Christian clichés on page 16. Can you think of other clichés you have heard when you have suffered a setback or tragedy in your life? Have they been hurtful or helpful?

5. Do you think there are different dynamics to consider when we pray for someone in person and when we pray for someone from a distance without their knowledge or consent? Could one kind of prayer be more effective than the other?

CHAPTER ONE

MY JOURNEY INTO PETITIONARY PRAYER

1. Lee Strobel put on his investigative hat to objectively examine the truth claims of Christianity. What are obstacles that may prevent people from being open-minded and fair when it comes to examining the effectiveness of prayer?

2. Have you ever carefully considered where your beliefs about prayer came from? What are the sources of your theology of prayer? Can you provide examples?

3. When building a theology of prayer, obviously the Scriptures are important. Are experience, reason, and science also appropriate tools for building a theology of prayer?

4. Does sitting alone in your room praying for God to stop gun violence, racism, or environmental pollution increase God's loving activity to stop those social ills? How so? Or why not?

5. Have you ever feared rejection by God, your family, or members of your church because of what you believe? Can you think of a time when you shared a difficult theological question and received judgment or criticism? Why do you think it is so difficult to question the status quo?

6. Within your church or denomination, what are doctrines that are considered okay to question? What are doctrines that are not okay to question?

7. Do you see prayer as speaking to a holy and transcendent Other? Or do you see prayer as more of a conversation with a friend? Define prayer in your own words.

8. Try this thought experiment. Let's assume you have been praying for your ailing relative. Repeat this sentence out loud: "I have been *praying* that God heals my _____." Now say, "I have been *talking* to God about healing my _____." Do you notice a difference between when you say "praying" and when you say "talking"?

9. What do you think it means to "pray without ceasing" (1 Thess 5:17)?

10. What do you think of this definition of petitionary prayer: *talking to God and asking God to love in a specific manner in which God was not doing so beforehand?* Do you agree with this definition?

CHAPTER TWO

WHAT ARE THE MECHANICS OF PRAYER?

1. E. M. Bounds, an author who is well-known for his many books on the topic of prayer, writes, "The concentration and aggregation of faith, desire, and prayer increased the volume of spiritual force until it became overwhelming and irresistible in its power." He goes on to say, "Units of prayer combined, like droplets of water, make an ocean which defies resistance."

   What do you think Bounds is talking about? What is the "volume of spiritual force"? What does he mean by "power"? What are "units of prayer"? Do they have something to do with mathematics? What does he mean by "an ocean which defies resistance"?

2. How does prayer work? In other words, what are the mechanics of prayer? What happens once your prayers leave your lips or after you speak them silently?

3. Some have suggested prayer releases and activates God's power. What does that mean? Do you believe that is the case?

4. When a person prays for God to heal their sick dad, does that give God extra power, energy, or motivation to do so?

5. Is persistent petitionary prayer performed simply to annoy God? Will God eventually and begrudgingly do the right thing and answer those prayers, as in the parable of the persistent widow and the uncaring judge (Luke 18:1–8)?

6. If an all-powerful God can single-handedly save and deliver people but allows them to get into fatal accidents, become sick, get raped, or experience other tragedies because others did not pray for them, can we call that God "loving"?

7. Define *theodicy* in your own words. In regard to theodicy, consider the difference between these two acts: praying to a God who automatically and single-handedly changes the outcomes of situations and the people in them and praying to a God who *cannot* coerce or control but requires cooperation to achieve loving outcomes.

8. What is your view of biblical inspiration? How do you think limited cultural understandings may have affected what the biblical writers say about God?

9. Do you think the biblical writers had a perfect understanding of prayer? Does the apostle Paul address the mechanics of prayer in his writings? Do you think Paul understood *how* prayer works?

10. Do you believe in *progressive revelation*? Why or why not? The doctrine of the Trinity developed over a period of centuries. Is it possible that our view of prayer could also evolve?

CHAPTER THREE

UNFORESEEN THEOLOGICAL AND PHILOSOPHICAL PITFALLS WITH PETITIONARY PRAYER

1. What do you think Jesus meant when he said, "When you pray, do not keep on babbling like pagans, for they think they will be heard because of their many words" (Matt 6:7)?

2. What is the point of praying if God already knows all about the situation we are praying for (Matt 6:8)?

3. Does petitionary prayer assume that God is not already performing or seeking to perform the requested action? Do you believe that praying for God to love, heal, and be gracious to loved ones suggests that God is not already loving, healing, and being gracious to them? Why or why not?

4. What is the hidden logic behind prayer chains? Does God wait until a certain number of people pray before answering the request? Would fifty people praying for Uncle Joe's sinus infection to be healed be more effective than one person praying?

5. Debbie prays on a daily basis, "God, pour out your love on Jason. Please save him." If God has always loved Jason and has always desired to save Jason—mind, body, and spirit—are Debbie's prayers in alignment with the reality of the profound goodness of God? Do her prayers make a good God look bad?

6. Read the illustration on page 55–56 about Sam's friend planning to visit a renowned Michelin-starred restaurant owned by Sam's relative. Do you think the friend's request for the chef to wash his hands before cooking and to kindly prepare a delicious meal is similar to asking God to extend love, grace, and mercy to loved ones? In what ways is it similar or different?

7. A Christian might pray, "God, pour out your love and save my child." Does this assume that God is withholding his love from that child and intentionally choosing not to save him or her? Is praying in this manner theologically consistent with God's loving nature and perfect will?

8. Do you believe God is in utmost control and that he has absolute power. If he chose to do so, could he single-handedly save people with complete disregard for their free will and agency?

9. Imagine a man watching a child being sexually assaulted. He has the power to do something about it but chooses not to because no one asks him. What do you think about such a man? Should we feel differently about God if he has full ability to intervene in horrific events and simply chooses not to?

10. If, on the one hand, God routinely intervenes in people's lives without specific prayers for them and, on the other, sometimes chooses to remain passive and do nothing simply because people haven't prayed, do you agree that the logical conclusion is that God is a cruel utilitarian, prioritizing the faith of some over the health of others, rather than a benevolent Father to all?

CHAPTER FOUR

CRITICAL EMPIRICAL AND EXPERIENTIAL CONCERNS ABOUT PETITIONARY PRAYER

1. Do you agree with *The New York Daily News*'s assessment that the politicians' prayers after the San Bernadino mass shooting were "meaningless platitudes"? When are prayers sincere, and when do they become mere platitudes?

2. What does it mean to say that petitionary prayer is effective?

3. Do you think the effectiveness of petitionary prayer can be proved empirically? If not, what do you believe are the obstacles to scientifically proving that petitionary prayer is effective?

4. Helen Parish and William Naphy define superstition as "an irrational, noncasual, and non-demonstrable connection between certain events, words, and actions and certain results." In what ways, if any, can petitionary prayer be superstitious?

5. Consider this sentence from the chapter: "If people believe that praying to God in a certain manner, at a certain volume, and with certain words will convince God to single-handedly root out prejudice, reduce hate crimes, solve the problem of homelessness, heal drug addicts, stop people from committing arson, stop rapes from occurring, and so on, they are engaging in magical thinking and superstition of the worst kind." Do you agree? Why or why not?

6. What is the biblical concept of *shalom*? What is God's primary method of achieving shalom on the earth? In what ways can petitionary prayer paradoxically become an obstacle to shalom?

7. James writes, "Faith by itself, if it is not accompanied by action, is dead" (James 2:17). Can the same be said of prayer?

8. Herbert and Catherine Schaible's two sick children died because they believed prayer would be enough to heal them. Can you think of a time when you have prayed fervently for someone's healing without taking it on yourself to be part of that healing? What might you have done differently?

9. Read Matthew 25:32–46. Does it surprise you that God's primary love language is service to others? What does that say about God's nature and character?

10. Why is it critical to take other variables, such as economic, political, and social factors, into account when talking about the topics of prayer, evil, and suffering?

CHAPTER FIVE
PETITIONARY PRAYER AND THE BIBLE

1. What is the difference between a wish and a prayer? Can you give an example of a wish in the Bible?

2. What do you think about prayer as spiritual warfare? Do you believe that your prayers somehow defeat demons? How so?

3. Jesus prayed, "Abba, Father, everything is possible for you. Take this cup from me. Yet not what I will, but what you will" (Mark 14:36). Do you think Jesus was intending to change God's mind? What was the purpose of Jesus's prayer?

4. What are *agonizing* prayers? Can you give a biblical example?

5. Paul writes about the agonizing prayers of Epaphras: "He is always wrestling in prayer for you, that you may stand firm in all the will of God, mature and fully assured" (Col 4:12). Did Epaphras think that because of his prayer, God would intervene unilaterally in the Colossians' hearts and increase the Colossians' maturity, assurance, and ability to stand firm in all the will of God?

6. What are your thoughts on the *Quadrilateral Hermeneutic of Love*? Is it an adequate lens to interpret a biblical writer's portrayal of God?

7. If the account in James about Elijah (5:17–18) is accurate and God singlehandedly brought about a drought that caused an enormous amount of suffering and death to plants, animals, and human beings, what does that say about God's character? What might be a different way to interpret God's role in the text?

8. What is your view of the inspiration of the Bible? Is every word dictated by God to the human authors? Does inspiration mean that every biblical author's view of God must be 100 percent accurate? What do you think of the analogy of the pants and the Bible on page 100?

9. If Acts 12 is to be read literally, then why is it that God is able to instantly and supernaturally send angels to break people out of prison without being seen and yet unable (or unwilling) to perform similar miraculous acts more frequently? Why doesn't God send angels more often to prevent people, including young children, from being raped? Since God can instantly flick open a massive iron gate, why doesn't he use his power to flick a psychopathic gunman in the head before a mass murder?

10. In Matthew 8 and Luke 7, Jesus uses his power and authority to heal the centurion's servant just by speaking a word. Are we to emulate Jesus's ability to heal others by praying on their behalf? Do you believe, like the centurion who displayed great faith, that we can pray for others and they will be instantly healed? If so, would you say that some people stay sick and perhaps even die because of a lack of faith and a lack of prayer?

CHAPTER 6
GOD'S PERFECT, UNCONTROLLING LOVE

1. Jesus tells his disciples and other curious spiritual seekers, "Love your enemies and pray for those who persecute you, that you may be children of your Father in heaven" (Matt 5:44–45). Whom do you consider to be your enemy? Pick one person, close your eyes, and consider praying for them. What thoughts and feelings come up for you?

2. Why do you think atheists in predominantly atheistic countries like China or Denmark experience the same "miracles" that praying Christians experience? In other words, why do atheists all of the sudden recover from illnesses, have money come in that they didn't expect, reconcile with family members, or get parking spaces close to the mall entrance, all without prayer?

3. Do you think that if God *is* love, then the biblical definition of love (1 Cor 13:4–8) must also be characteristic of God? Likewise, is the fruit of the Spirit (Gal 5:22–23) characteristic of the Spirit?

4. The Scriptures say God cannot lie (Heb 6:18), cannot be tempted (Jas 1:13), cannot be prejudiced (Acts 10:34–35), cannot sin (Deut 32:4), and cannot get tired (Isa 40:28). Can you list some other things that God *cannot* do?

5. Thomas Oord says that God *never* unilaterally controls but always works in cooperation with others. What do you think of Oord's notion of God's uncontrolling love?

6. Oord writes, "Because love is the preeminent and necessary attribute in God's nature, God cannot withdraw, override or fail to provide the freedom, agency, self-organizing and lawlike regularity God gives. Divine love limits divine power." In what ways does love limit divine power? Can you provide biblical examples?

7. Do you believe God is doing all he can do to maximize good and minimize evil? Is God constrained by other variables, such as human free will?

8. In William Young's *The Shack*, Papa responds to Mack's pain and his burning questions regarding the brutal murder of his daughter. Papa says, "This was no plan of Papa's. Papa has never needed evil to accomplish his good purposes. It is you humans who have embraced evil and Papa has responded with goodness." Do you agree with Young's characterization of God?

9. Does randomness, or as William Hasker puts it, "chanciness," occur in the world? Or is every event that occurs uniquely *planned* or *allowed* by God? Discuss the difference between *planned* and *allowed*.

10. What kind of world would we live in if there were no possibility of choice, pain, and evil? Would we experience less of what we consider beautiful and good as a consequence of living in such a world? What kind of world would we live in if God forcefully stopped every evil before it occurred?

CHAPTER 7
GOD'S OPEN-DOOR POLICY

1. Is it true that the traditional model of petitionary prayer tends to ask God to love or change others without taking into consideration other dynamics and agencies, such as a person's free will?

2. The Bible says, "Without faith it is impossible to please God, because anyone who comes to him must believe that he exists and that he rewards those who earnestly seek him" (Heb 11:6). What does faith and an *Open-Door Policy* have to do with prayer, especially in relation to having prayers answered?

3. Consider this statement: "God will not intervene unilaterally, bypassing the will of people in a controlling manner to root out hatred and oppressive tendencies, even if we petition and plead with him to do so." Do you agree? Why or why not?

4. What thoughts and feelings come up when you consider the possibility that God is not in control of every event that occurs?

5. What comes to mind when you think of God's power? Is God's power forceful? Or is it non-coercive? Does suggesting that God cannot unilaterally control people or singlehandedly change the course of events diminish God's power?

6. Jesus, the all-powerful, mighty God, met people he couldn't heal (Mark 6:5). What does that say about God's power? What implications does it have for our prayers?

7. There are many Christians who are bogged down by the weight of shame because they look at others who are healed and ask, "Why not me?" They conclude something is wrong with their faith, with their prayer life, or with their character. Would it help them to understand that human agency is not the only agency that God is responding to and that other non-human agencies could potentially become an obstacle to people's healing?

8. Can you describe the difference between *basic needs* and *discretionary needs*?

9. Let's say a friend of yours on Facebook posted, "Can you pray that God would comfort my brother and his wife? They lost their child and are in desperate need of God's grace." Will praying alone in your room, "God, please comfort my friend's family and extend your loving mercy and grace to them," increase God's comfort, mercy, and grace in their lives?

10. Consider the similarities between praying to God that he would comfort and pour out his grace on a family affected by a traumatic event and asking someone to do the dishes while they are in the middle of doing the dishes. Is it better to ask God, "How can I join you in extending your comfort and grace to them?" just as it is better to ask the person, "Hey, can I help you with that?"

CHAPTER 8
PRINCIPLES OF CONSPIRING PRAYER

1. What does it mean for *conspiring prayer* to be prayed *with* God instead of *to* God? How are conspiring prayers subversive?

2. How is praying, "God, my heart longs for you to save and deliver my dad," different in the traditional model of prayer and the conspiring model?

3. If you knew that because God's nature is love, he couldn't single-handedly control events and instantly give you what you wanted, would you still pray as often to God and share your heartfelt requests?

4. Do you agree that prayers for such needs as more love, more peace, less violence, healing from injury or illness, salvation, the eradication of hunger and poverty, and the healing of our planet are already a "Yes and Amen" to God?

5. What does it mean to listen *with* God? What is the difference between listening with God and having a conversation with people?

6. Have you ever heard the voice of God? Do you think God speaks audibly? If God can speak to us audibly but chooses not to even when he might warn us and keep us from harm, what does that say about God's character?

7. If it is necessary to listen with God to achieve God's unique mission in the world, then why is it so hard? What are common obstacles to listening with God?

8. What is the difference between engaging in social justice with God and doing so apart from God?

9. Why is gratitude so important in conspiring prayer? How can we thank God even in the midst of evil?

10. Consider this statement: "The sovereignty of God, when misunderstood by Christians as 'God is in control of everything,' is one of the most detrimental, devilish doctrines and deterrents to human flourishing that I know." Do you agree?

CHAPTER 9
CONSPIRING PRAYER IN ACTION

1. In what ways do you and your church already engage in conspiring prayer?

2. What are some obstacles to engaging in conspiring prayer in your church?

3. What are some deficits of the conspiring prayer model? How could it be improved for your unique context?

4. Are "You do it, God" types of prayers as transformative as "How can we do it, God?" types of prayers?

5. How can silence with God rid the heart of idolatry?

6. It is common for Christians to pray, "God, please give the doctors wisdom," when sick or hurting loved ones are in the hospital. Would it be more effective to pray with the doctors in their presence? Or would praying for them from afar be just as effective?

7. Tamar Manessah, a divine echo, listened to God in prayer, heard his creative instruction, obeyed, and became a force of light and love thwarting gang violence on a small street corner in Chicago. Think about a person or crisis that needs the tangible love of God. Close your eyes and listen with God. Can you hear God whisper a mission that he wants you to be a part of?

8. How would you engage in petitionary prayer directly after a mass shooting? In the past, how have you prayed after hearing about a mass shooting? Now that you're familiar with conspiring prayer, how might you pray after such events in the future?

9. God is not a cruel scriptwriter who plans for people to have mental illness. He is doing all he can do to free them and heal them. Does this thought provide you solace? Or does the fact that God is not controlling and cannot heal without cooperation from people and lawlike regularities provoke anxiety?

10. What kind of world would we live in if Christians and churches prayed conspiring prayers and became divine echoes in the world? Would there be any difference?

APPENDIX 1

WRITE YOUR OWN CONSPIRING PRAYER

- READ SOME OF THE PRAYERS IN THE APPENDIX.

- SIT IN PRAYERFUL SILENCE.

- THINK OF A POPULATION OR CRISIS THAT IS IN NEED OF THE GRACE, HEALING, AND LOVE OF GOD.

- KEEP A FEW THINGS IN MIND:
  - GOD'S LOVE IS UNCONTROLLING.
  - GOD IS WITH YOU AND WITHIN YOU; HE LOVES YOU AND DESIRES SHALOM FOR WHATEVER YOU PRAY FOR.
  - GOD'S DESIRE FOR US AS THE CHURCH IS TO BE DIVINE ECHOES, PARTNERING WITH HIM TO BRING FORTH SHALOM IN THE WORLD.

- HUMBLY ASK GOD TO INSPIRE YOU.

- BE CREATIVE, SPEAK FROM YOUR HEART, AND WRITE YOUR PRAYER.

- SHARE IT WITH OTHERS.

For more information about Mark Gregory Karris
or to contact him for speaking engagements,
please visit *www.markgregorykarris.com*

Many voices. One message.

Quoir is a boutique publishing company
with a single message: Christ is all.
Our books explore both His
cosmic nature and corporate expression.

For more information, please visit
www.quoir.com

www.ingramcontent.com/pod-product-compliance
Lightning Source LLC
Chambersburg PA
CBHW081357080526
44588CB00016B/2526